ALWAYS TO REMEMBER

The Story of the Vietnam Veterans Memorial

ALWAYS
TO
REMEMBER

The Story of the Vietnam Veterans Memorial

Brent Ashabranner

Photographs by Jennifer Ashabranner

SCHOLASTIC INC.
New York Toronto London Auckland Sydney

ISBN 0-590-44590-1

Text copyright © 1988 by Brent Ashabranner. Photographs copyright © 1988 by Jennifer Asha-branner. All rights reserved. Published by Scholastic Inc., 730 Broadway, New York, NY 10003, by arrangement with G.P. Putnam's Sons, a division of The Putnam Berkeley Group Inc.

12 11 10 9 8 7 6 5 4 3 2 1   2 3 4 5 6/9

Printed in the U.S.A.   23

First Scholastic printing, January 1992

For

Peggy O'Callaghan

And to the memory of her brother, whose name
is on the Vietnam Veterans Memorial

1959

IN HONOR OF THE MEN AND WOMEN OF
THE ARMED FORCES OF THE UNITED
STATES WHO SERVED IN THE VIETNAM
WAR. THE NAMES OF THOSE WHO GAVE
THEIR LIVES AND OF THOSE WHO REMAIN
MISSING ARE INSCRIBED IN THE ORDER
THEY WERE TAKEN FROM US.

· BRIAN J O'CALLAGHAN

OUR NATION HONORS THE COURAGE
SACRIFICE AND DEVOTION TO DUTY AND
COUNTRY OF ITS VIETNAM VETERANS.
THIS MEMORIAL WAS BUILT WITH
PRIVATE CONTRIBUTIONS FROM
THE AMERICAN PEOPLE.
NOVEMBER 11, 1982

1975

Panel # W 14

Line # 39

◆ Contents

ALWAYS TO REMEMBER

The Story of the Vietnam Veterans Memorial

◆ Memorial Day

CONSTITUTION GARDENS is a lovely park on the Mall in Washington, D.C. Cars stream by on Constitution Avenue, one of the busiest thoroughfares in the nation's capital, but the park is shielded from noise by a long line of trees. On the western edge of the park stands the white marble temple of the Lincoln Memorial. On the eastern edge the Washington Monument pierces the sky. Between these treasured landmarks lie the sweeping lawns and grassy knolls of Constitution Gardens. Near the park's center is a small lake where ducks swim. The bolder ones cruise near the edge, alert for crusts of bread thrown by picnickers and government workers having their brown-bag lunches in the sun. The park is a peaceful place in a throbbing, noisy city.

On a day in May, Memorial Day, I went early in the morning to Constitution Gardens. I walked down the path to the lake and circled to the south edge of the park near the reflecting pool where the Washington Monument's image almost touches the Lincoln Memorial. I followed the path up a long incline through rows of trees and stopped

A part of Constitution Gardens, only a minute's walk from the Vietnam Veterans Memorial.

Park police on horses help maintain the peaceful atmosphere of Constitution Gardens.

when I came to the three infantrymen in battle dress. They are cast in bronze, these battle comrades, but they seem alive, and my eyes followed their gaze down the grassy slope to the black granite panels which form a long, tapered wall at the bottom of the hill.

It is angled to form a wide *V*, this wall. It seems to rise out of the earth and recede back into it. I had been to this place many times, and my feeling today was the same as it had always been—that I was seeing the wall for the first time. Perhaps it is the feeling of discovery; for if you did not know it was there, in this quiet park, you would have to stumble onto it by accident. Perhaps it is the knowledge of what it is that you can never get used to.

This wall is the Vietnam Veterans Memorial, of which the bronze statue of the soldiers and a nearby American flag are a part. Into the polished granite have been cut the names of over 58,000 servicemen and women who died in the Vietnam War or who still are missing. Line after line, panel after panel, the names stretch from the intersection of the two halves of the wall for nearly 250 feet in each direction, one pointing toward the Lincoln Memorial, the other toward the Washington Monument. On one of the center panels is etched a brief tribute: "Our nation honors the courage, sacrifice and devotion to duty and country of its Vietnam veterans."

But the names themselves, in a seemingly endless litany in stone, provide their own heartbreaking message: in war young men die. Young women die in war, too; the names of eight nurses are on the wall. But the call of war has always been a call for young men. The average age of the men who died in the Vietnam War was nineteen.

"I wept," said writer James J. Kilpatrick, describing his first visit to the Vietnam Veterans Memorial. "The memorial carries a message for all ages: this is what war is all about."

IN THE truest sense every day at this name-filled wall is a memorial day. Visitors come to the memorial from all over the country. They come at

These army fatigues belonged to one of the names on panel 44E of the memorial.

all times of day and night, at all times of the year, in all kinds of weather. They come to stand silently before the wall, to search for a name, to touch a name, to place a flower, a message, or a memento close to a name etched in the black granite. Since the memorial was dedicated in 1982, it has become the most-visited memorial or monument in Washington.

Today, the day set aside each year for America to officially honor its war dead, would be no different except for the formal ceremony at midday. Although it was only a little after dawn, people were already at the wall, and others had been there before them. Already tokens of love were accumulating at the base of the memorial.

The western side of the wall points toward the Lincoln Memorial.

Left: *The eastern side of the wall points toward the Washington Monument.*

Flags, flowers, and mementos are placed at the base of the memorial every day of the year by visitors.

I walked from the center of the wall, first to the east toward the Washington Monument, then to the west toward the Lincoln Memorial. Many single yellow roses had been placed in front of the wall. A note taped to a scuffed baseball said, "Teddy, people still talk about your fastball. Mom and I are always thinking about you. Dad." A handwritten card leaning against the wall said, "Death ends a life, not a relationship." It was signed with a woman's name.

As I moved slowly past the flowers and floral wreaths that were placed beneath almost every panel of the wall, I recalled that Memorial Day had once been called Decoration Day because it is the day when graves of the war dead all across America are decorated with flowers by those who remember them. I recalled that one mother, speaking of the Vietnam Veterans Memorial, had said, "This is my son's tombstone."

The inscription on this plaque reads: "Lt. Col. Fred V. Cole, the best Battalion Commanding Officer anyone could ask for . . . God Bless You, Sir."

Once I had heard a young girl ask her father, "Are they buried here?"

Her father was a soldier in uniform. "No," he said, "they're buried in their hometowns. But they're together here."

The mother and the soldier were both right.

I stopped to read a note impaled on the handle of a miniature flag. The note was addressed to two names on the wall. "I should have been with you guys," it said. "I'll see you guys in heaven 'cause we spent our time in hell."

Once I had asked myself if it was right to read these messages left at the wall. I had decided that it was. They were expressions of private grief, but something told me the persons who left them wanted to share their grief with others, to reach out to others who felt the same emotions.

By noon several thousand people were at the memorial. Many walked slowly past the memorial wall as I had. Some sat or stood on the grassy slope in front of the memorial. Others gathered around the statue of the three soldiers. The mood was solemn, but here and there I saw smiles and heard laughter as Vietnam veterans met, exchanged greetings, and talked. Hundreds of Vietnam veterans were at the memorial, many wearing faded army fatigues. Some who were seeing the names on the wall for the first time did not try to keep back their tears.

At one o'clock the Memorial Day program began. Jan Scruggs was master of ceremonies, as he is at almost every ceremony at the memorial. The idea of a national memorial with the names of all Americans who died in Vietnam had first been his, and he had never turned loose of the idea until it was a reality.

Scruggs introduced John Wheeler, board chairman of the Vietnam Veterans Memorial Fund, who talked about the healing that was still taking place in America, a healing of wounds caused by the bitter controversy over the war. The Vietnam Veterans Memorial had helped in the healing, he said. He talked about the 157 other memorials to

Christmas memories.

Easter morning.

Right: *The elaborate remembrance reads: "Beloved son, brother, brother-in-law, and uncle."*

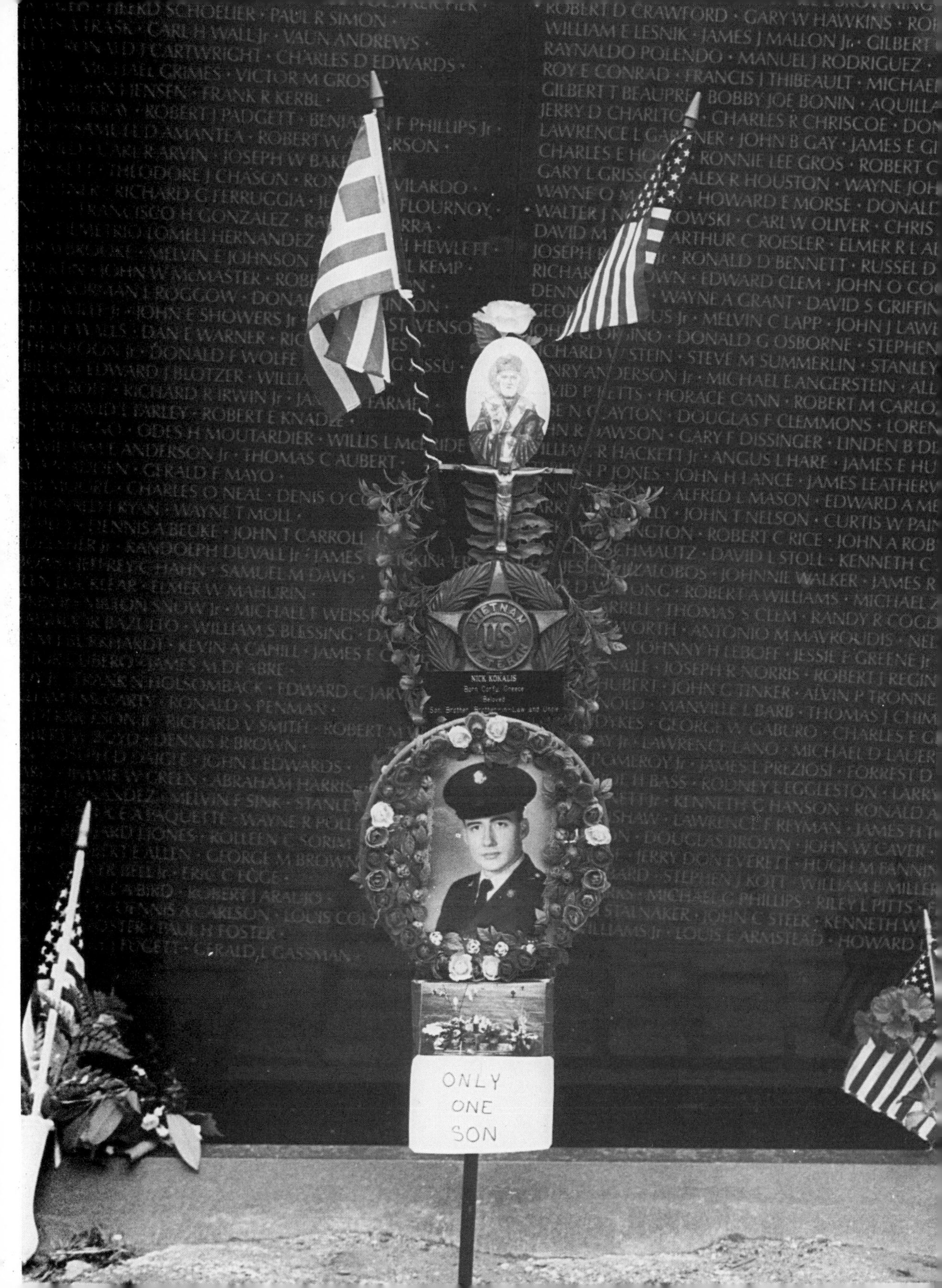
NICK KOKALIS
Born Corfu, Greece
Beloved
ONLY
ONE
SON

Before entering the priesthood, Father Charles Fink was an infantryman in the Vietnam War.

Vietnam veterans, smaller local memorials, that had been built or were now being built in other parts of the country. They were helping in the healing, he said.

Wheeler noted that many children are among the millions of visitors who come to the Vietnam Veterans Memorial in Washington every year. Children, Wheeler said, ask the tough questions. Who were these people whose names are on the wall? How old were they? Why did they die?

Father Charles Fink, a Catholic priest, said a prayer and talked about the war in Vietnam. Seventeen years ago, ten years before he became a priest, he had been a combat rifleman in Vietnam.

"I hated the war," he said. "Some days I still can almost smell the jungle and rice paddies. Now I am a Catholic priest, and I hate war. But nothing makes me so proud as to have served with those men."

Behind the priest was the black wall of the memorial bearing the names of some of those with whom he had served.

After the program part of the crowd left, but other visitors came to the memorial. Late in the afternoon I watched a man and woman and their son—he was perhaps ten or eleven years old—as they walked slowly along the memorial wall. After a while the boy trailed behind, stopping to read every plaque, to look at every medal, to examine every token of remembrance that had been placed at the wall.

Before the boy caught up with his parents, he took something out of his pocket and placed it beneath one of the panels of the wall. After he was gone, I went to look at what he had put there. It was a small blue marble.

◆ A Nation Confused and Divided

BEFORE the mid-1950s probably not many Americans knew much about Vietnam. The small Southeast Asian country, together with Cambodia and Laos, was an Indochinese colony of France. But after World War II a burning desire for independence swept over the countries of Africa and Asia that for generations had been dependencies of European countries. In some cases the change from colony to independent country was achieved with a minimum of bloodshed. In other cases, European countries stubbornly resisted loss of their African and Asian territories.

The French fight to keep control over Vietnam lasted nine years, but in 1954 the French army suffered a terrible defeat at a place called Dien Bien Phu. The Vietnamese independence fighters, called Vietminh (Vietnam Independence League), were made up of Communists and non-Communists who put aside their political differences to fight the French. Until the final siege at Dien Bien Phu, they employed hit-

and-run tactics known as guerrilla warfare, attacking French forces, then using jungle, mountains, and rural countryside to escape.

After the French defeat at Dien Bien Phu, a conference was held in Geneva, Switzerland, in 1954, attended by a number of countries, including the United States; different Vietnamese factions attended. At the conference Vietnam was divided into Communist North Vietnam and nationalist South Vietnam. Nationwide elections were to be held later to decide whether the entire country would have a Communist or non-Communist government.

The South Vietnamese regime, however, refused to hold the elections, and in 1955 declared South Vietnam an independent republic. Immediately, North Vietnam began to support Communist groups, called Vietcong, in South Vietnam, and the Vietnam War was underway. The Vietcong used the same guerrilla tactics that the Vietminh had used against the French.

In 1955 the United States began to help South Vietnam, and for ten years sent military advisers and billions of dollars in war equipment and economic aid to that country. But the Vietcong, aided by North Vietnam, remained a constant threat to the government in the south. In 1965 President Lyndon Johnson sent the first American combat troops to South Vietnam, and at that point the Vietnam War became principally an American war.

The war in Vietnam bitterly divided America. Millions of Americans believed that our support of non-Communist South Vietnam was necessary to prevent the expansion of Communism in Southeast Asia. They thought that if Communist North Vietnam took over South Vietnam, other Southeast Asian countries such as Thailand, Indonesia, and the Philippines would topple like a row of dominoes in the face of advancing Communism. This belief was known as the domino theory.

But to millions of other Americans, the United States should never have been fighting a war in Asia, a war that necessitated moving troops and material halfway around the world. They believed that we had no business interfering in what they felt was a Vietnamese internal matter.

19

Groups of Vietnam veterans exchanging greetings and memories are a common sight at the memorial on Veterans Day, Memorial Day, and the Fourth of July.

Whether all of Vietnam became Communist, they contended, was for the Vietnamese to decide, no matter what the United States thought of the decision.

If U.S. involvement in Vietnam had lasted only a short time, these differing points of view might not have intensified and hardened as they did. But the Vietnam War was not short. To the contrary, it became the longest war in United States history, and the number of American troops in Vietnam increased steadily. By the end of 1965, 200,000 American fighting men were in Vietnam; by 1966 that number had doubled. Within a year the number reached half a million. Still the Vietcong remained strong in South Vietnam, and the deadly guerrilla war in jungles and rice paddies did not slacken. Americans were fighting and dying, but victory did not seem to be anywhere in sight.

U.S. military leaders continued to insist that the war was winnable and asked for still more troops to be sent to Vietnam. But millions of Americans believed that Vietnam had become a bottomless pit for American men and equipment. By 1967 massive antiwar demonstrations were taking place in the United States. Candlelight peace marches attracted thousands in major cities. Draft cards were burned in public protest rallies.

President Johnson was unwilling to further increase troop strength in Vietnam, but he was unable to find a way to end the war without admitting defeat. In a tacit admission of failure, he announced that he would not seek reelection as president. In the presidential campaign of 1968 that followed, Richard Nixon narrowly defeated Democratic Vice President Hubert Humphrey. Although he was not specific, Nixon said he had a plan to end the war that would bring the United States "peace with honor."

But the war in Vietnam went on for over four years after President Nixon took office. Finally, in 1973, a cease-fire agreement was signed in Paris. Most U.S. troops returned home. In April, 1975, the Army of North Vietnam, ignoring the cease-fire, invaded South Vietnam and routed the South Vietnamese Army. The few remaining American armed forces and embassy personnel made a last-minute escape from Vietnam. Finally, the war was over.

The cost of the war to America was staggering:

- Over 58,000 servicemen and women killed or missing.
- More than 300,000 wounded, 74,000 of these crippled with a more than 50 percent disability.
- $140 billion spent. This did not include future billions that would be spent on wounded and disabled veterans.

There were other costs in shattered or permanently marred lives. Over 7,500 young American men were sent to prison for refusing to serve in the military. A shocking 425,000 men deserted from military service from 1966 to the end of the war. Most of these had surrendered or been caught and punished, but 32,000 were still at large.

RREN P NIX • STEPHEN V PARKER • SAMUEL L
EZ • GEORGE W PICKEL • WILLIAM D POOLE
OMAS W SADLER • RALPH M SANTINELLO • M
AM V SPRINGFIELD • WESLEY W STEVENS • JEF
ARPE • ALBERT C THOMPSON • JAMES M THO
UA • JAMES R WALTERS • ALAN C WARD • JOH
N J WIESER • RAYMOND L WILLIAMS • KENNE

A Canadian flag at the memorial. About thirty thousand Canadians—sometimes called "the unknown veterans"—joined the United States armed forces and fought in the Vietnam War.

The cost in human lives to South Vietnam was terrible: 200,000 soldiers killed, an estimated half million civilians killed. North Vietnamese costs were higher, an estimated one million killed in combat. Civilian casualty figures for North Vietnam are unknown.

Another cost of the war, even after it ended, was the continuing dissension in the United States about what should or should not have happened. The United States had never before lost a war. The "hawks" or "hardliners" maintained that we would not have lost in Vietnam if the military had been fully supported in its call for more combat troops and had been allowed to use all the weapons it had, including tactical nuclear weapons.

Those who opposed the Vietnam War—the "doves"—continued to feel that it was a war that should never have been fought, that we had nothing to gain from fighting in Southeast Asia and no moral right to be there. They pointed out as evil and immoral the kinds of weapons used: defoliants (Agent Orange) that destroyed all plant and animal life over thousands of square miles, napalm that burned people to death, and massive aerial bombardment that top U.S. officials said would bomb North Vietnam "back to the Stone Age." No victory was worth those atrocities, they said, and they did not bring victory.

With this dissension came a loss of national confidence and common purpose that the American people had never before experienced, but there seemed to be no way to reconcile points of view so different.

Another tragic outcome of the war was the treatment of Vietnam veterans upon their return to America. The veterans of earlier American wars had been welcomed home as heroes with ticker-tape parades, speeches of appreciation, and the friendly smiles and support of everyone who saw them in uniform. Not so with the veterans of the Vietnam War. America was sick of the cost and dissension of a war it did not win. And by 1973 the country was totally focused on the Watergate scandal of the Nixon administration. Most Vietnam veterans were at best ignored; many met outright hostility.

The memorial is an emotional meeting place for thousands of Vietnam veterans.

Left: *"Heroes in Black Stone," a song about Vietnam veterans and the many kinds of people who visit the memorial, was sung by Glenn Garrett on Veterans Day, 1986.*

Former senator and presidential candidate George McGovern was a bitter critic of the Vietnam War, but speaking of Vietnam veterans (as quoted in the *Washington Post*), he had this to say: "I was treated as a hero when I got home from World War II, but I was not any braver than those who served in Vietnam, and we almost sneaked them in under the cover of darkness. Their psychological needs are more acute than those of veterans of any other war the United States has been involved in."

Mr. McGovern was right about the bravery of those who fought in Vietnam. Countless stories of heroism under fire in Vietnam have been recorded, but no story tells as much about combat courage than this one statistic: 24 percent of all Marines who were sent into battle in Vietnam were killed or wounded. That is the highest casualty rate in Marine Corps history.

Over 2.5 million American men and almost 8,000 women served in Vietnam between 1964 and 1975. Another million served in Southeast Asian countries outside of Vietnam. Government estimates are that as many as 800,000 Vietnam veterans suffered from emotional stress or disorders of varying degrees of seriousness. Most veterans worked their way through their emotional problems, which were given the name post-Vietnam traumatic stress, but their adjustment doubtless would have been easier in an understanding, comforting environment.

Dazed, hurt, angry, unappreciated, unable to communicate, Vietnam veterans were by any definition casualties of the war.

◆ Jan C. Scruggs:
The Nightmare and the Dream

H E WAS like a million others who went to Vietnam, just out of high school, no real idea of what he wanted to do. Most of his friends were going to college and would be deferred from the draft. He didn't have any thought of going to college, not then; his parents couldn't afford to send him. Besides, he felt in a vague way that joining the army was a good idea, a good thing to do for his country.

His name was Jan Scruggs, and he was nineteen in 1969 when he was sent to Vietnam and assigned to the 199th Light Infantry Brigade. He was in Vietnam for over a year, and in that time he saw over half of his company killed or wounded. He spent one terror-filled night pinned down by North Vietnamese machine-gun fire. He and others in his squad lived through that night because one man in the squad exposed himself to enemy fire and certain death for the few precious minutes the squad needed to retreat with their wounded.

Later Scruggs was wounded. He came back to America with shrapnel still in his body and in his mind the memory of carrying lifeless comrades through the mud of Vietnam. He hardly returned to a hero's welcome. Antiwar feeling in the United States was still intense, and Scruggs remembers being booed when he and some of his army companions, still in uniform, walked down the street.

Back in his hometown of Bowie, Maryland, almost a suburb of Washington, D.C., Scruggs, now twenty, still didn't know what he wanted to do. He worked for a while as a security guard at an apartment complex, then drifted around the country for several months with a friend. After that he returned to Bowie and enrolled in the local community college. Later he transferred to American University in Washington and took a master's degree in psychology and counseling.

No matter where Scruggs was, thoughts of Vietnam did not go away. While studying at American University the idea of a memorial to Vietnam veterans first came to him. America wanted to forget the Vietnam War, but it shouldn't forget. A memorial to the men and women who lost their lives in Vietnam would help the country remember. And maybe, Scruggs thought, a memorial might help lessen the war bitterness that still divided Americans.

But in 1977 those thoughts were only the dreams of a college student who had no idea of the planning, organization, money, political knowledge, and friends that would be needed to change a dream into reality.

In early 1979, married and working now for the U.S. Department of Labor, Jan Scruggs saw a movie called *The Deer Hunter*. It is a powerful story of Americans in the war in Vietnam. The movie upset Scruggs, shook him badly. After he got home from the theater, he couldn't sleep. He stayed up most of the night, and scenes of his own Vietnam experiences began to flash in his head.

"It was just like I was in the army again and I saw my buddies dead there," Scruggs said, years later. "Twelve guys, their brains and intestines all over the place. Twelve guys in a pile where the mortar rounds had come in."

The morning after that night of terrible memories, Scruggs told his wife that he was going to build a memorial to all of the men and women who had been killed in Vietnam. "All their names will be there," he said.

Jan Scruggs was not much more qualified then to lead a drive to build a memorial to Vietnam veterans than he had been as a college student, except in one way. Now it was not just a vague idea. Now he was determined to do it.

"I became obsessed," Scruggs said.

And that made the difference.

But how do you build a national memorial? Who designs it? What should it look like? Where do you put it? How much does it cost? Where does the money come from? Those were just some of the questions that began to spin through Scruggs's head as he stayed up late night after night for weeks after he made up his mind that somehow, some way a Vietnam Veterans Memorial would be built.

People told Scruggs that his idea wouldn't work. They said the war was still too much an emotional issue for people to support a memorial. The government would never appropriate money for it. Besides, memorials take time; they can't be rushed. The Washington Monument took a hundred years to complete. The Lincoln Memorial wasn't finished until fifty years after Lincoln's death. After twenty-five years Congress still couldn't reach agreement about a memorial for President Franklin D. Roosevelt.

Scruggs listened, but he had answers to all of those objections. He didn't intend to build a memorial to the Vietnam War but rather to the men and women who fought and died in the war. There was a big difference. And Scruggs didn't want government money to build the memorial. As he saw it, the money would come as contributions from private citizens all over the country. As for taking twenty-five or fifty years to build—well, that just couldn't happen. The memorial was needed now, not sometime in the next century.

At a meeting of Vietnam veterans in Washington, Scruggs tried to explain his ideas about a memorial, but he got the same kind of "it can't

Jan Scruggs at microphone on Memorial Day, 1987. The woman is interpreting through sign language for the hearing impaired.

be done" answers. After the meeting, however, one of the veterans came up to Scruggs and told him that the first thing he should do was form a nonprofit organization, a Vietnam Veterans Memorial Fund, that could develop plans for the memorial and receive tax-exempt contributions. The veteran who gave Scruggs that advice was Robert Doubek, a Washington lawyer who had been an Air Force officer in Vietnam. From that moment Doubek became a supporter of the memorial idea, and his support never wavered.

Scruggs sold a tiny piece of land he owned in order to get start-up money, then filed the papers necessary to legally register the Vietnam Veterans Memorial Fund. Scruggs knew nothing about holding press conferences, but he held one now to announce that a memorial to the men and women killed or missing in the Vietnam War would be built. He asked for contributions and support from private citizens.

Scruggs held his conference on May 28, 1979. Exactly ten years earlier, May 28, 1969, he had been pinned down by mortar fire and wounded in a jungle in Vietnam.

Newspapers around the country carried stories about Scruggs's idea of building a Vietnam veterans memorial with private contributions. Many people wrote to Scruggs praising the idea. Letters came from all kinds of people but mostly from veterans, parents who had lost sons in Vietnam, and wives and children of veterans. Many of the letters spoke bitterly of the lack of recognition and help those who fought the war had received.

Several million dollars would be needed to build the memorial, and Scruggs watched the post office box anxiously in the days and weeks after the wire services carried stories about the memorial idea. But only a trickle of money came with the letters, and after a month the Vietnam Veterans Memorial Fund had received just $144.50. Television commentators and comedians made jokes about the financial "support" the memorial idea was receiving.

Other things began to happen, however. One of the most important was a phone call Scruggs received from John Wheeler, a Vietnam veteran who heard about the Memorial Fund's money-raising problems and volunteered to help. Wheeler quickly became crucial to changing the memorial from dream to reality. Like Doubek, he was a Washington attorney, a graduate of the Yale Law School and also of the Harvard Business School. In addition to those impressive credentials, Wheeler had graduated from West Point and, before resigning his commission, had served as an officer in Vietnam.

Wheeler knew influential people in the business world, the military, government, and the legal profession. He got in touch with some of those people, and he, Scruggs, and Doubek met with them to talk about the memorial and try to get their help. Out of these meetings came capable volunteers for the organizational, publicity, and fund-raising tasks of the Vietnam Veterans Memorial Fund and valuable supporters in the corporate and professional worlds.

While he now had an impressive team around him, Scruggs was from first to last the leader. The task he set for himself was one of the biggest and most important: to get the support of Congress. Before a Vietnam Veterans Memorial could be built on public land in Washington, the Senate and House of Representatives had to pass a bill approving such a memorial, and the president had to sign the bill.

As a Maryland citizen, Scruggs went first to see the senior senator from Maryland, Charles McC. Mathias, Jr. Some people might have questioned that choice since Senator Mathias had been a consistent opponent of American involvement in Vietnam throughout the years of conflict there. But the senator, with the wisdom that made him one of Washington's most respected political figures, was able to distinguish between the war and those who fought it. He listened, got full details about the Vietnam Veterans Memorial Fund, and became a leading supporter in Congress.

Scruggs, Doubek, and Wheeler carried out a vigorous campaign to win other support in Congress, and their success was spectacular. In the end twenty-six senators cosponsored a bill authorizing the Vietnam Veterans Memorial Fund to build a memorial on public grounds in Washington, D.C. The bill was also heavily cosponsored in the House of Representatives, and it passed both houses of Congress unanimously. On July 1, 1980, President Jimmy Carter signed the bill, and it became effective as Public Law 96-297.

The new law contained several details of great importance. The most exciting was that it pinpointed the location of the Vietnam Veterans Memorial on the Mall in the area known as Constitution Gardens; it further specified a placement near the Lincoln Memorial. In their most optimistic dreams Scruggs and his fellow officers of the Fund had never believed that such a location was possible. On the Mall and next to the Lincoln Memorial! Usually the site of a memorial or monument in Washington is left up to the Commission of Fine Arts and the National Capital Planning Commission, but the idea of putting the Vietnam Veterans Memorial near the Lincoln Memorial belonged to

Trees and gentle grassy slopes make the memorial a peaceful place in the midst of a busy city.

Senator Mathias, and such was his stature in Congress that his fellow legislators supported the idea.

The law specified that "neither the United States nor the District of Columbia shall be put to any expense in the establishment of the memorial." The law further stated that construction of the memorial had to begin within five years but that it could not be started until enough money was on hand to complete it.

All of those conditions were fine with the Vietnam Veterans Memorial Fund board of directors. Although most people thought their timetable was a joke, they were determined to have the memorial built and ready for dedication by Veterans Day, 1982—just a little over two years away!

Collecting money to build the memorial—always a high priority— now became the top priority. A national sponsoring committee contained such names as First Lady Rosalyn Carter, former President Gerald Ford, and General William Westmoreland, commander of U.S. forces in Vietnam through much of the conflict. Bob Hope signed a contributions-request letter that went to tens of thousands of American homes. The American Legion, Gold Star Mothers, Veterans of Foreign Wars, and other organizations began to publicize the Vietnam Veterans Memorial Fund's need for cash contributions.

Some wealthy Americans such as Texas billionaire H. Ross Perot and Senator John Warner made large contributions to the memorial fund. But finally it was thousands of unwealthy Americans, sending in amounts of $1, $5, $10, and $20, who donated most of the millions of dollars finally needed to build the memorial.

◆ The Vision of Maya Ying Lin

T HE MEMORIAL had been authorized by Congress "in honor and recognition of the men and women of the Armed Forces of the United States who served in the Vietnam War." The law, however, said not a word about what the memorial should be or what it should look like. That was left up to the Vietnam Veterans Memorial Fund, but the law did state that the memorial design and plans would have to be approved by the Secretary of the Interior, the Commission of Fine Arts, and the National Capital Planning Commission.

What would the memorial be? What should it look like? Who would design it? Scruggs, Doubek, and Wheeler didn't know, but they were determined that the memorial should help bring closer together a nation still bitterly divided by the Vietnam War. It couldn't be something like the Marine Corps Memorial showing American troops planting a flag on enemy soil at Iwo Jima. It couldn't be a giant dove with an olive branch of peace in its beak. It had to soothe passions, not stir them up. But there was one thing Jan Scruggs insisted on: the memorial, whatever it turned out to be, would have to show the name of every man and woman killed or missing in the war.

"These names, seemingly infinite in number . . ."—Maya Lin

The answer, they decided, was to hold a national design competition open to all Americans. The winning design would receive a prize of $20,000, but the real prize would be the winner's knowledge that the memorial would become a part of American history on the Mall in Washington, D.C. Although fund raising was only well started at this point, the choosing of a memorial design could not be delayed if the memorial was to be built by Veterans Day, 1982. H. Ross Perot contributed the $160,000 necessary to hold the competition, and a panel of distinguished architects, landscape architects, sculptors, and design specialists was chosen to decide the winner.

Announcement of the competition in October, 1980, brought an astonishing response. The Vietnam Veterans Memorial Fund received over five thousand inquiries. They came from every state in the nation and from every field of design; as expected, architects and sculptors were particularly interested. Everyone who inquired received a booklet explaining the criteria. Among the most important: the memorial could not make a political statement about the war; it must contain the names of all persons killed or missing in action in the war; it must be in harmony with its location on the Mall.

A total of 2,573 individuals and teams registered for the competition. They were sent photographs of the memorial site, maps of the area around the site and of the entire Mall, and other technical design information. The competitors had three months to prepare their designs, which had to be received by March 31, 1981.

Of the 2,573 registrants, 1,421 submitted designs, a record number for such a design competition. When the designs were spread out for jury selection, they filled a large airplane hangar. The jury's task was to select the design which, in their judgment, was the best in meeting these criteria:

- a design that honored the memory of those Americans who served and died in the Vietnam War.
- a design of high artistic merit.
- a design which would be harmonious with its site, including visual harmony with the Lincoln Memorial and the Washington Monument.
- a design that could take its place in the "historic continuity" of America's national art.
- a design that would be buildable, durable, and not too hard to maintain.

The designs were displayed without any indication of the designer's name so that they could be judged anonymously, on their design merits alone. The jury spent one week reviewing all the designs in the airplane

"The area contained within the memorial is a quiet place, meant for personal reflection and private reckoning."—Maya Lin

hangar. On May 1 it made its report to the Vietnam Veterans Memorial Fund; the experts declared Entry Number 1,026 the winner. The report called it "the finest and most appropriate" of all submitted and said it was "superbly harmonious" with the site on the Mall. Remarking upon the "simple and forthright" materials needed to build the winning entry, the report concludes:

> This memorial with its wall of names, becomes a place of quiet reflection, and a tribute to those who served their nation in difficult times. All who come here can find it a place of healing. This will be a quiet memorial, one that achieves an excellent relationship with both the Lincoln Memorial or Washington Monument, and relates the visitor to them. It is uniquely horizontal, entering the earth rather than piercing the sky.
>
> This is very much a memorial of our own times, one that could not have been achieved in another time and place. The designer has created an eloquent place where the simple meeting of earth, sky and remembered names contain messages for all who will know this place.

The eight jurors signed their names to the report, a unanimous decision.

When the name of the winner was revealed, the art and architecture worlds were stunned. It was not the name of a nationally famous architect or sculptor, as most people had been sure it would be. The creator of Entry Number 1,026 was a twenty-one-year-old student at Yale University. Her name—unknown as yet in any field of art or architecture—was Maya Ying Lin.

How could this be? How could an undergraduate student win one of the most important design competitions ever held? How could she beat out some of the top names in American art and architecture? Who was Maya Ying Lin?

The answer to that question provided some of the other answers, at least in part. Maya Lin, reporters soon discovered, was a Chinese-American girl who had been born and raised in the small midwestern city of Athens, Ohio. Her father, Henry Huan Lin, was a ceramicist of considerable reputation and dean of fine arts at Ohio University in Athens. Her mother, Julia C. Lin, was a poet and professor of Oriental and English literature. Maya Lin's parents were born to culturally prominent families in China. When the Communists came to power in China in the 1940s, Henry and Julia Lin left the country and in time made their way to the United States.

Maya Lin grew up in an environment of art and literature. She was interested in sculpture and made both small and large sculptural figures, one cast in bronze. She learned silversmithing and made jewelry. She was surrounded by books and read a great deal, especially fantasies such as *The Hobbit* and *Lord of the Rings.*

But she also found time to work at McDonald's. "It was about the only way to make money in the summer," she said.

A covaledictorian at high school graduation, Maya Lin went to Yale without a clear notion of what she wanted to study and eventually decided to major in Yale's undergraduate program in architecture. During her junior year she studied in Europe and found herself

Carolou Marquet

Maya Lin at First Day ceremony for Vietnam Veterans Memorial Commemorative stamp. Others in picture (from left) Brigadier General George Price, Postmaster General William F. Bolger, Jan Scruggs, John Wheeler.

"*A memorial shouldn't tell you what to think, but it should make you think.*"
—*Maya Lin*

increasingly interested in cemetery architecture. "In Europe there's very little space, so graveyards are used as parks," she said. "Cemeteries are cities of the dead in European countries, but they are also living gardens."

In France, Maya Lin was deeply moved by the war memorial to those who died in the Somme offensive in 1916 during World War I. The great arch by architect Sir Edwin Lutyens is considered one of the world's most outstanding war memorials.

Back at Yale for her senior year, Maya Lin enrolled in Professor Andrus Burr's course in funerary (burial) architecture. The Vietnam Veterans Memorial competition had recently been announced, and although the memorial would be a cenotaph—a monument in honor of persons buried someplace else—Professor Burr thought that having his students prepare a design of the memorial would be a worthwhile course assignment.

Surely, no classroom exercise ever had such spectacular results.

After receiving the assignment, Maya Lin and two of her classmates decided to make the day's journey from New Haven, Connecticut, to Washington to look at the site where the memorial would be built. On the day of their visit, Maya Lin remembers, Constitution Gardens was awash with a late November sun; the park was full of light, alive with joggers and people walking beside the lake.

"It was while I was at the site that I designed it," Maya Lin said later in an interview about the memorial with *Washington Post* writer Phil McCombs. "I just sort of visualized it. It just popped into my head. Some people were playing Frisbee. It was a beautiful park. I didn't want to destroy a living park. You use the landscape. You don't fight with it. You absorb the landscape . . . When I looked at the site I just knew I wanted something horizontal that took you in, that made you feel safe within the park, yet at the same time reminding you of the dead. So I just imagined opening up the earth. . . ."

When Maya Lin returned to Yale, she made a clay model of the vision that had come to her in Constitution Gardens. She showed it to

Professor Burr; he liked her conception and encouraged her to enter the memorial competition. She put her design on paper, a task that took six weeks, and mailed it to Washington barely in time to meet the March 31 deadline.

A month and a day later, Maya Lin was attending class. Her roommate slipped into the classroom and handed her a note. Washington was calling and would call back in fifteen minutes. Maya Lin hurried to her room. The call came. She had won the memorial competition.

◆ Approval and Groundbreaking

J AN SCRUGGS was not an artist, sculptor, or architect. When he first saw Maya Lin's design, he thought it looked like a bird, a big black bat, maybe. He was puzzled. And then he saw the names—a wall of names of all the men and women who had died in the Vietnam War. That was what he had wanted from the beginning, and there they were. And they would be on the Mall forever.

The Vietnam Veterans Memorial Fund accepted the competition jury's recommendation. The National Capital Planning Commission and the Commission of Fine Arts approved both the memorial's design and its proposed location near the Lincoln Memorial. Fine Arts Chairman J. Carter Brown said that Maya Lin's design had an "extraordinary sense of dignity and nobility."

The stage now seemed set for the last act: the actual building of the memorial. But that was not the case. While there was wide support for Maya Lin's memorial design, almost at once critical voices began to be heard. Some veterans and others who had strongly supported the idea

44

of a Vietnam veterans memorial—including H. Ross Perot—simply did not like the design that had been chosen.

They called it "unheroic." They were troubled by the fact that it would be built into the ground, in effect become a part of the earth, and that black granite would be used for the panels. One protester, appearing before the Commission of Fine Arts, called the proposed memorial "a black gash of shame." Why couldn't white marble be used? some critics wanted to know. Why couldn't it be built aboveground? Some people just didn't understand it. It was abstract, modern art. They wanted a traditional memorial with human figures—soldiers, airmen, nurses—symbolizing the years of service and sacrifice in Vietnam.

One member of the selection jury had been prophetic when he had said, "Many people will not comprehend this design until they experience it."

Maya Lin said, "I hope they will give it a chance and not close their minds."

She was hurt because people accused her of making a political statement about the Vietnam War. In a letter of protest to President Reagan, a group of congressmen called her memorial design a statement of "shame and dishonor." The truth is that Maya Lin knew very little about the Vietnam War, a fact she readily admitted. She was a baby when serious U.S. involvement in Vietnam began; she was fourteen years old when the last American troops left that country. The Vietnam War protests of the sixties and seventies had not been a part of her life. To her, the memorial she had designed honored those who had died in Vietnam, but it also was symbolic of the sacrifice and sorrow that is a nation's burden in any war.

There were answers to the other objections. Maya Lin had chosen black granite partly because of its superb reflective quality; it would give back to those who visited the memorial images of themselves as well as reflections of trees, sky, and earth. Besides, sunlight would have made white marble so dazzlingly bright that the names could not have been read. As for its being built aboveground, the effect of comfort and

45

The polished black granite of the memorial wall gives back mirror sharp reflections of people, earth, sky, trees, the Washington monument, and the Lincoln Memorial.

Right: *". . . this memorial is for those who have died, and for us to remember."—Maya Lin*

security Maya Lin wanted would have been lost entirely; also, an aboveground structure would detract from the Lincoln Memorial, only six hundred feet away.

Black is the traditional color of sorrow; but the argument that it was the color of shame came to a quick halt after General George Price, one of the military's highest-ranking black officers, took the floor in a public meeting about the memorial. Black was not the color of shame, he said. He reminded the veterans that color meant nothing when they were fighting in Vietnam.

"Color should mean nothing now," he said.

Support for the memorial design chosen by the Vietnam Veterans Memorial Fund poured in—both cash contributions and praise—from individuals and organizations all over the country. The American Legion supported it. The Gold Star Mothers supported it. Editorials in important newspapers gave it their endorsement and said the construction should proceed. But the opponents had powerful influence in Congress, and they had the ear of James Watt, the Secretary of the Interior. His signature on a construction permit was necessary before the memorial could be built on the Mall, and he showed no signs of giving his approval. He was listening to both sides and waiting.

As the clash of ideas continued into early 1982, the Vietnam Veterans Memorial Fund board became desperate. If construction did not begin soon, the memorial would never be ready for dedication on Veterans Day in November. Furthermore, the Fund was planning a national salute to Vietnam veterans to be held as part of the dedication. Announcements had already gone out, and tens of thousands of Vietnam veterans were expected to pour into Washington for the dedication of the memorial. Disaster loomed if there was no memorial or if it wasn't ready for dedication.

On January 27, a long and tense meeting took place between Jan Scruggs and other members of the Vietnam Veterans Memorial Fund and some of the most vocal and powerful critics of Maya Lin's design. After four hours they were in as much disagreement as they had been at

48

The flag is a part of the Vietnam Veterans Memorial.

the beginning; the whole idea of a memorial for Vietnam veterans was now very much in doubt.

General Michael Davison, adviser to the Fund and former commandant of West Point, was at the meeting. At a moment when things looked most hopeless, he stood up. Why not, he asked, make a statue of a serviceman as part of the memorial? In retrospect, the suggestion seems like a simple and logical compromise, yet in the months of bitter quarreling, no one had thought of it. Up to that moment, it had been either-or: either leave the memorial just as Maya Lin had conceived it or change it completely, perhaps scrap it for something entirely different.

Honor guard at memorial groundbreaking.

Left: *Groundbreaking for the memorial, March 26, 1982.*

General Davison's idea probably saved the Vietnam Veterans Memorial or at least prevented a delay of years in its construction. The critics of Maya Lin's design were willing to compromise on the addition of a statue—and an American flag—as a part of the memorial. The Vietnam Veterans Memorial Fund agreed to the additions and commissioned Frederick Hart, a Washington sculptor, to create the bronze statue.

At first Maya Lin was upset by the possibility of anything being added to the memorial wall she had conceived. She was afraid that if a statue was placed above the wall or directly in front of it, the effect she envisioned would be ruined. When it became clear, however, that the statue and flag would be placed at some distance from the wall, she did not object further.

Some people said that a lifelike statue could not be combined effectively with the abstract art of the black granite wall. But that remained to be seen, and Scruggs and his colleagues were willing to take that risk in order to get the memorial built on schedule. The statue could not be sculpted and cast in time for the dedication on Veterans Day, but it could be added later. At last Secretary Watt gave his approval for the memorial to be built.

Groundbreaking ceremonies for the Vietnam Veterans Memorial were held on March 26, 1982. The day was cold, sunny, a stiff breeze snapping the flags of the military honor guard. Shovels were laid out on the ground, one for every state, one for every veterans organization at the ceremonies. Many emotional speeches were made, but the words of Army Chaplain Max D. Sullivan perhaps came closest to expressing the hope of Scruggs, Doubek, Wheeler, and the many others who had labored so mightily to make this moment possible: "May this be a holy place of healing for the conflicting emotions of that terrible, divisive war . . ."

Shovels bit into the earth; the ground was broken; the building of the Vietnam Veterans Memorial had begun.

After an unusual snowstorm, the dark wide V of the memorial stands out dramatically against the white landscape.

◆ The Memorial Is Built and Dedicated

T HERE WAS everything to do and not much time to do it; Veterans Day, the target date for dedicating the memorial, was less than eight months away. The Fund hired an architectural firm to draft precise plans for Maya Lin's design, a contractor to prepare the land and build the memorial, and a landscape architect to make certain that the memorial grounds were in harmony with the rest of the park. Maya Lin took leave from Yale to be a consultant to the project. She was not yet an architect and had not been trained in drafting, but she had a vivid mental image of what the memorial and its setting should look like.

Bulldozers moved earth to form a wide, sloping *V* in a Constitution Gardens hillside near the Lincoln Memorial. Concrete pilings, 140 in all, were sunk into the ground to form a solid base to support the granite wall. Granite for the wall was quarried in southern India. The fine-grained Indian granite, when polished, would gleam like a black mirror.

The granite came from India as large, thick slabs. These were trucked to the town of Barre, Vermont, where a stonecutting company sliced them into panels and polished the panels to a high luster. Each side of the memorial, both east and west, would be made up of seventy panels. The panels would vary from a height of about ten feet at the center, where the two sections meet, to eight inches, where they end. The fabrication of each side—making it a unified whole by properly cutting and shaping each panel—was a task requiring the highest stoneworking skill.

After the panels were cut to proper size and polished, they were shipped to Memphis, Tennessee, where the names of the Vietnam War dead and missing were added. The process was a complex one. The Defense Department furnished a computer tape of Vietnam War casualties, checked and rechecked. Photographic stencils of the names, arranged not alphabetically but by date of death, were placed on the panels. The names were then sandblasted onto the panels by hand.

In her design description, Maya Lin had been very specific about the order in which the names should be inscribed on the wall. The names should begin and end in the center where the two halves of the wall meet. The name of the first person killed in the Vietnam War (1959) should be inscribed at the top of the east side, and names would then follow chronologically—in order of date of death or date declared missing—to the end of the east side. The chronological listing would then begin again at the end of the west side, and the names would continue in order of date of death until the name of the last person killed (1975) was inscribed at the bottom of the west side.

"Thus," Maya Lin wrote, "the war's beginning and end meet; the war is 'complete,' coming full circle . . ."

The memorial was completed in a frenzy: fitting the panels together, laying the walkways, recontouring the land, resodding the soil. But the job was done in less than eight months; and the whole Vietnam Veterans Memorial project—from the moment Jan Scruggs announced the idea in a press conference until the last black granite panel was in

The Vietnam Veterans Memorial under construction, summer, 1982.

National Park Service Photo

Each name is preceded on the west side of the wall or followed on the east side of the wall by a diamond or a cross. A diamond means that the serviceman or servicewoman's death has been confirmed. The cross means that the person was missing at the end of the war and is still unaccounted for. The names of 1,300 missing servicemen are on the wall. If a death is confirmed, the cross will be changed to a diamond. If a missing man returns alive, a circle—as a symbol of life—will be inscribed around the cross.

place—took less than three-and-a-half years. This was a record in national memorial building that may never be equaled.

VETERANS DAY honors the men and women who have fought in every American war, but in Washington, D.C., the 1982 Veterans Day ceremonies had a special emphasis on Vietnam veterans. The Vietnam Veterans Memorial Fund organized a Salute to Vietnam Veterans that would last from November 10 through November 14 and would include the dedication of the Vietnam Veterans Memorial on November 13.

Over 150,000 Vietnam veterans poured into Washington from all over the country. Most of them found it hard to believe that such a salute

Park rangers helping visitors find names in the location directory.

could take place. They had come to believe that America would never show any appreciation to the veterans of that long and unpopular war.

The five-day program began with a moving candlelight vigil in honor of Americans killed or missing in Vietnam. During the vigil, held in Washington Cathedral, volunteers read the names of the dead and missing. Volunteers also read Protestant, Roman Catholic, Jewish, and Unitarian prayers. As they read names and offered prayers, the volunteers stood beside a wooden altar set with candles and white chrysanthemums. The reading of the 57,939 names (the number of known dead and missing at that time) began Wednesday morning at ten o'clock and continued without interruption until midnight on Friday.

Many other activities took place during the five-day salute. Reunions of military units were held. The American Red Cross, Gold Star, and many other organizations held open house receptions. Entertainers, including actor Jimmy Stewart and singer Wayne Newton, put on a salute program. The U.S. Army Band played a concert.

Saturday morning, November 13, a Tribute to Vietnam Veterans Parade was held in the streets of Washington. The marchers included veterans, military units, marching bands, and others. Crowds lined the streets and cheered. For many of the Vietnam veterans, perhaps for most, this was the first time they had heard such cheers.

At two-thirty that afternoon the Vietnam Veterans Memorial was dedicated. Jan Scruggs, Robert Doubek, and John Wheeler sat on the speakers' platform and listened to the cheers of the thousands who surrounded the memorial. They had done the impossible, and they knew they had done it well.

TWO YEARS later, Veterans Day, 1984, the bronze statue of the three servicemen was installed and dedicated. Again the crowd was huge, and this time President Reagan attended the ceremony and accepted the completed memorial for the nation. "I believe that in the decade since Vietnam the healing has begun," the president said, "and I hope that

Park rangers and Friends of the Vietnam Veterans Memorial will give visitors blank forms for making name rubbings.

before my days as Commander in Chief are over the process of healing will be complete."

The statue quickly won the hearts of almost all who saw it. Although realistic to the smallest detail, the realism does not detract from the abstract memorial Maya Lin designed, as many had feared it would. The three soldiers are not "heroic," but the fatigue of battle shows in their faces and in their weary posture. By an inspired placement of the statue, the three men seem to have emerged from a clump of trees atop the hill. They have sighted the black wall in the distance and seem to be looking at the names inscribed there.

Are they looking for the names of comrades? Are they looking for their own names?

Left: *The statue of the three servicemen is remarkable for its realism, with every detail of battle dress and weaponry accurate to the smallest detail. The three figures clearly suggest different racial and ethnic backgrounds. Sculptor Frederick Hart says, "The portrayal of the figures is consistent with history. They wear the uniform and carry the equipment of war; they are young. The contrast between the innocence of their youth and the weapons of war underscores the poignancy of their sacrifice."*

These worn and tattered, but freshly washed, fatigues were placed at the memorial on the Fourth of July, 1987.

◆ A Special Place

In the years since its dedication, the Vietnam Veterans Memorial has become a special place in many ways to many people. The memorial's unique emotional appeal is most poignantly revealed in the way visitors bring cherished mementos of the past and leave them in front of the black stone wall.

Once I made a visit to the National Park Service's Museum Archeological Regional Storage Facility (MARS) in Lanham, Maryland. Here is stored material belonging to forty National Park Service locations such as the Jefferson Memorial, Harper's Ferry, and Mount Vernon. Here also are kept memorabilia left at the Vietnam Veterans Memorial.

When the memorial was built, no one foresaw that parents, relatives, friends would bring mementos and messages to the wall and leave them, but this unusual act of communication began early and has grown every year since the dedication of the memorial. Today storage cabinets and shelves at MARS contain thousands of items that have been placed at the base of the memorial and left there.

David Guynes, curator and site manager of MARS, showed me around the huge warehouse. About a third of all items left at the memorial are military, he told me: identification tags, clothes, ribbons, medals. Bronze Stars, Distinguished Flying Crosses, many Purple Hearts, one Medal of Honor have been left. A little less than one-third of the items are written material: letters, one-line notes, cards, poems, messages from schools and churches. The large remaining miscellaneous category is made up of toys, books, phonograph records, many things that had value and meaning only for the persons who put them there and to the names on the wall that they had belonged to—a yellow plastic duck, a high school class picture, a tennis racket with well-worn grip and broken string.

"Everything but organic material—flowers, wreaths—that's left at the memorial is collected by park rangers for storage at MARS," Guynes said. "The ranger enters the item in a log with the date and time of day recorded. He puts down the number of the memorial panel where the item was placed. At MARS the item is given an inventory number. We list the ranger who collected the item. Then we store it in whatever is the best way for that particular item."

I was impressed, but I couldn't help asking, "Why do you do all this, save all these things?"

Guynes must have been asked that question many times, but he was silent for several moments before he answered. Then he turned, opened a cabinet full of toys and stuffed animals and took out a small, worn teddy bear lying in a shallow white box. Guynes is a big man with powerful hands, but they held the teddy bear gently, as if it needed special care. Clearly, to him it did.

"This was one of the early mementos left at the memorial," he said. "A mother and father whose son's name is on the wall put it there. They left a greeting card, too, and a photograph of a 1955 car. Newspaper articles were written about the bear, and the parents identified themselves. They were interviewed on Ted Koppel's 'Nightline' television program. They said they had bought the bear for their son in 1938

David Guynes

One of the mysteries David Guynes spoke of. The name on this display is that of a
man who apparently died in 1987. The word "Guadalcanal," suggests that he
served in the Pacific in World War II. Is his son's name on the memorial wall?

when he was a baby. They wanted to return it to him. The car in the photo was his first car."

Guynes put the teddy bear back in the storage cabinet. "It's one of the few things we have here at MARS that we have good background on," he said. "Things left at the memorial."

And then Guynes answered my question. "Most museums, most curators, carefully select what is to make up their collection," he said. "That's not the case here. We must collect everything. There are so many questions, so many mysteries, in these memorabelia. So many stories are in them, so much feeling, emotion, heartache. What can be learned about America and Americans from these things they have brought? Altogether, these materials make up a very important part of the story of the Vietnam War."

Guynes looked around at the tables, shelves, and storage cabinets. Perhaps it was my imagination, but his eyes seemed to glow. "This is the material of social history," he said.

MARS is not open to the public, though someday, on some limited basis, it may be. Guynes and his small staff zealously protect the collection from abuse. None of the written material may be read or copied. It is Guynes' hope that in time the most qualified historians, psychologists, and anthropologists will have access to the collection, under professional conditions.

MY NEXT visit to the memorial after my trip to MARS was on a softly warm evening in June, one of those rare times when Washington's climate can match that of any place in the world. A full moon was rising in the southern sky, but the strong twilight would hold for another two hours. I had come to the memorial thinking it might be a quiet time, but I should have known better. Even this early in summer, tourist season was in full swing in Washington, and the evening hour made no difference to the large crowds.

Another mystery at the memorial wall. What is the meaning of the torn dollar bill placed with these U.S. Marine Corps clothes?

Right: *Reading American "social history."*

The tranquil, contemplative atmosphere that Maya Lin envisioned for the memorial did not exist at a time like this. Hundreds of people streamed down the walk in front of the granite wall. On Constitution Avenue and near the Lincoln Memorial tour buses deposited large groups of summer visitors. To them the Lincoln Memorial and the Vietnam Veterans Memorial were a combined stop on a busy two or three days of planned sightseeing that would include at least a dozen other major stops: the Capitol, the White House, the Library of Congress, the Washington Monument, and on and on.

The first time or two that I had seen tour groups at the memorial, I had had mixed feelings. This kind of mass visiting wasn't right, I told myself, making a tourist attraction out of the memorial. But as I watched I saw that they weren't really groups. Almost at once they broke up, some looking for a specific name, some reading the messages at the base of the memorial, a few making rubbings of names, some just standing quietly, looking at the names. For most of these people the only way they would ever be able to visit the memorial was as a part of a tour group. Why shouldn't they come? They should, of course.

Tonight a man and woman from one of the groups sat down on a bench beside me near the statue of the three soldiers. They were from a town in Ohio, the man told me, and this was their first trip to Washington, something they had wanted to do for years. The man's wife was holding a red carnation.

"Is a relative's name on the wall?" I asked, not wanting to say son.

"No," she said, "but our neighbor's son is there. She asked us if we would try to find his name."

They had looked up the location of the name on the wall, and I walked down with them. The woman took a note from her purse and pushed the stem of the carnation through it. Then she placed the flower and note at the base of the panel. The note said, "Dear Bill, I would be there if I could. Love, Mom."

David Guynes is right, I thought, as I left the memorial that night. A little bit of America's social history is written here every day.

Tracing a name on the wall is a continual activity at the memorial.

THE Vietnam Veterans Memorial is special in the different faces it shows at different times of day, the different moods it evokes at different times of year. At dawn, when the first sunlight turns the white marble of the Lincoln Memorial a soft pink, the black granite wall becomes warm with the light. At night the ground lights shining on the names seem comforting and the nearby Washington Monument, awash with light, is reassuring.

When snow blankets the ground, the black granite gleams with reflected whiteness and casts an almost hypnotic spell on anyone

Finding a name on the wall and touching it is an act repeated hundreds of times each day.

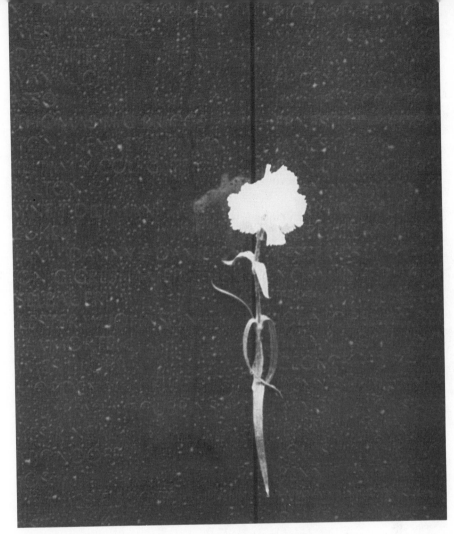

Rain like tears on the memorial wall, Veterans Day, 1986.

standing before the wall. In spring when the grassy knolls of Constitution Gardens turn green and the encircling trees are in leaf, the memorial, which is a part of the earth, seems most peaceful.

Rain brings its own special mood, usually a mood of melancholy. On Veterans Day, 1986, a cold, steady drizzle began falling from a gray November sky. Raindrops glistened like tears on the black wall of the memorial. But the mood of melancholy was lessened on this Veterans Day by something special: a magnificent 15 × 25-foot American flag atop the memorial wall. The flag was made up of 58,132 red roses, white carnations, and blue bachelor buttons, a flower for every name on the wall. Like the Vietnam Veterans Memorial itself, the flag of flowers was the dream of one person, a Virginia woman named Victoria Richards; also like the memorial, many people had helped her dream come true.

Months before this Veterans Day, Victoria Richards, a housewife and mother of two children, had been watching Chuck Norris, the actor, on a television talk show and had learned that Norris's brother had been killed in Vietnam. Mrs. Richards was moved by Norris's obvious pain in talking about his brother's death. She decided to visit the Vietnam Veterans Memorial and place a flower by the dead brother's name. She did not know his first name, however, so was unable to locate the correct panel at the memorial.

But while she was there, she saw a man in army fatigues place a flower at the base of the memorial, and it was then that she had her idea. There were thousands of people all over the country who would like to place a flower beside the name of a loved one on the wall if they could only be there. Why not place a flower at the memorial—a rose—for every name inscribed there. She began to think of her idea as "A Rose of Remembrance." The roses would symbolize the persons who could not be at the memorial in person, and they would symbolize the names on the wall.

As her thinking developed, the big question was, how do you arrange nearly sixty thousand flowers—three pickup trucks full, she was told!—in front of the memorial? Her idea of a flag of flowers solved the problem, and the need for red, white, and blue flowers instead of all red roses took shape.

Mrs. Richards received support for her idea from Senator John Kerry, Senator John Warner, Jan Scruggs, and others. She got in touch with Chuck Norris who offered to help in any way he could, but Mrs. Richards told him that she just wanted his moral support. The planning and fund raising took months, but help came from many sources. A

A rose of remembrance.

number of corporations gave money for the flowers; Fred Smith, a Vietnam veteran and owner of Federal Express, furnished an airplane to bring the flowers from California and Colorado.

The day before Veterans Day, a Washington florist, Angelo Bonita, and his staff began work on the giant floral arrangement. Dozens of other volunteers, many of them Vietnam veterans, helped build the frame for the flag and cut the stems off the thousands of flowers. They worked through the night in a big white tent on the Mall near the memorial, and by the time the first visitors arrived the next morning, the flag of flowers was in place above the memorial wall.

Victoria Richards at dedication of the flag of flowers.

Honor guard and flag of flowers, Veterans Day, 1986.

By one o'clock, the time for the Veterans Day program, drizzle had changed to a steady rain. The crowd had grown throughout the morning despite the rain, but many wondered if the program would be postponed. A cheer went up when Jan Scruggs stepped to the microphone promptly at one and asked, "Did they ever call off the war for rain?"

Massachusetts Senator John Kerry on Veterans Day, 1986. "This wall and this day remind all who served and came home of a special responsibility we have to avoid any glorification of war."

Senators Kerry, Warner, and Edward Kennedy all spoke. Senator Kerry was a Vietnam veteran, but after his discharge, he helped create an organization, Vietnam Veterans Against the War, to have a voice in the war protest. Kerry talked about the controversy and said, "For a long time, America did not distinguish the war from the warrior, and so the warrior suffered a wrongful neglect. This wall and this day cry out to remind America that no matter how unpopular the war itself, the soldiers who fought and served did so with as much passion, as much commitment and love of country as at any other moment in this nation's history."

80

Referring to Victoria Richards and her work, Senator Kerry said, "Behind us is an extraordinary flag of flowers, the culmination of the dream of one individual to pay her tribute.

"Finally," the senator concluded, "this wall and this day remind all who served and came home of a special responsibility we have to avoid any glorification of war."

Chuck Norris was on the speakers' platform, sitting next to Victoria Richards. He had arrived in Washington the day before and had spent much of that day at the memorial talking to veterans. Standing before the wall bearing the names of all the Vietnam War dead—including his

Actor Chuck Norris (center) at memorial, Veterans Day, 1986. The name of Norris's brother, Wieland, is on the memorial.

brother, Wieland Norris—Chuck Norris spoke of those who came back from the war, the veterans.

"For ten years these men were treated like traitors," he said. "Now we are trying to make up for it."

MOST SPECIAL of all is the closeness of the Vietnam Veterans Memorial to the Lincoln Memorial. The Lincoln Memorial is the nation's most revered monument. From his massive white marble chair in this temple, Lincoln looks out across the Mall to the Capitol in the distance. And now, since 1982, his gaze falls first on the Vietnam Veterans Memorial only six hundred feet away. The closeness of the two memorials means that almost everyone who visits one goes to the other.

Lincoln brought the nation through a war more bitter and divisive than the Vietnam War. On one of the walls of his memorial is engraved his Second Inaugural Address to the nation. The final words of the great address carry a powerful message for the person who has just come from or who is about to go to the Vietnam Veterans Memorial:

> With malice toward none, with charity for all,
> with firmness in the right as God gives us to see the right,
> let us finish the work we are in,
> to bind up the nation's wounds,
> to care for him who shall have borne the battle,
> and for his widow and his orphans,
> to do all which may achieve and cherish a just and a
> lasting peace among ourselves and with all nations.

In winter, the Lincoln Memorial is more clearly visible through the leafless trees.

◆ Always to Remember

TODAY THE Vietnam Veterans Memorial does many things. It sends a message to all veterans of that war that their effort and their sacrifice are now acknowledged and appreciated. It sends the same message to those who lost a son, a husband, a father, a brother, a friend in Vietnam. It provides a place where all Americans, no matter what their feelings about the war, can meet on the common ground of sorrow and respect for those who gave their lives.

But, finally, the purpose of a memorial is to keep remembrance alive. The time will come when no person who visits the Vietnam Veterans Memorial will have known anyone whose name is on the wall. I asked Jan Scruggs and Maya Lin what they thought the memorial will mean to future generations.

"I think it will make people feel the price of war," Scruggs said, emphasizing the word "feel." "I think it will make them understand that the price has to be paid in human lives.

84

Over eight million children have visited the memorial since its dedication.

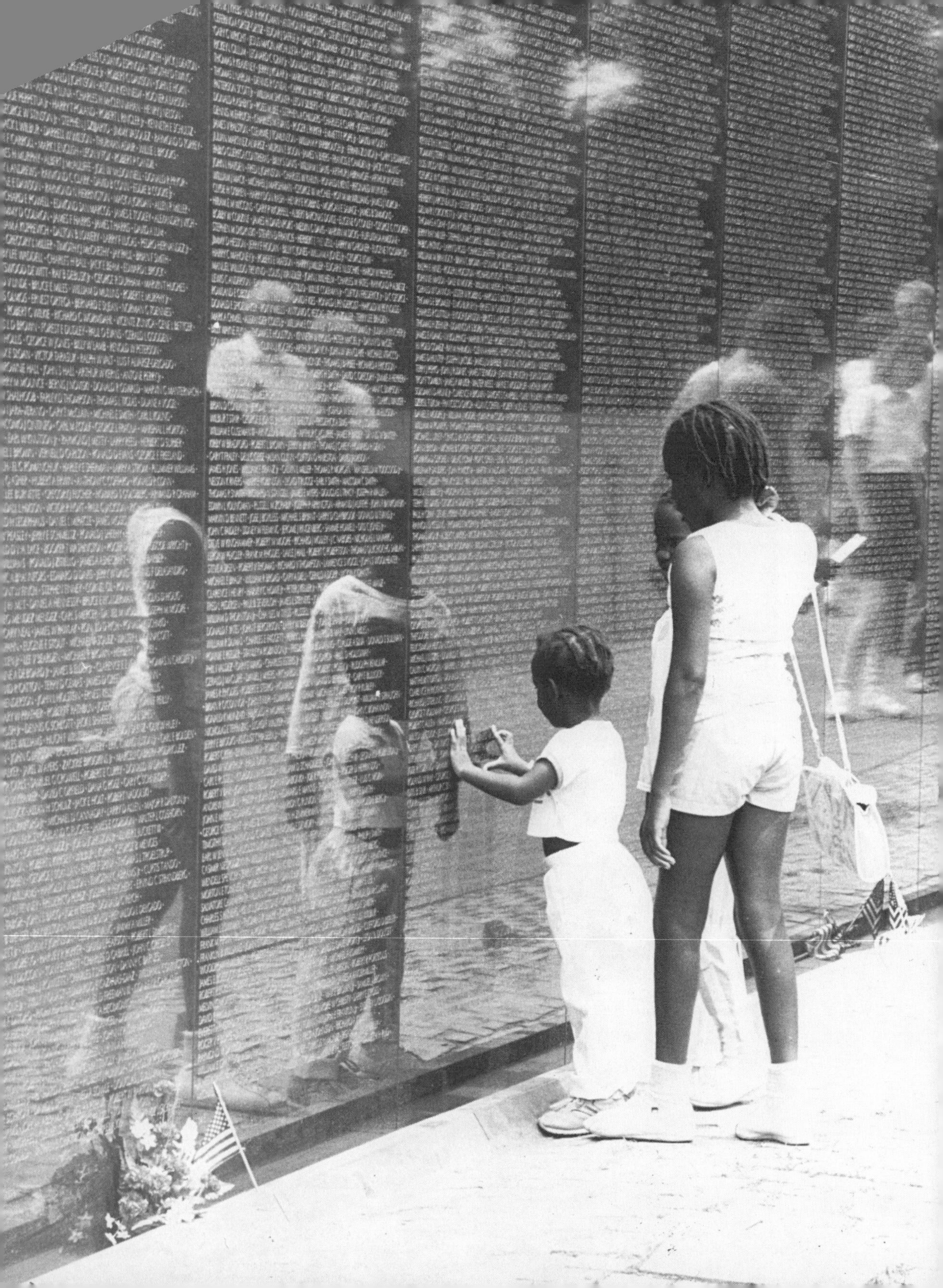

"I hope it will make people think about the national leaders they elect, leaders who will keep the country out of war if possible but fight it hard if there has to be war." Scruggs paused and then said, "I think the memorial will say, 'In a war young men and women have to serve their country.'"

Maya Lin commented, as she had in the past, that the message of the memorial—to any person, any time—will depend on the feelings, the background, the life experiences that the person brings to it. "It will always be a private, personal thing," she said. "But the memorial will always be about loss and about the price of war."

I agree with Jan Scruggs and Maya Lin. By its somber beauty, by its placement in our nation's capital between the Lincoln Memorial and the Washington Monument, the Vietnam Veterans Memorial will make us remember that at a certain time, in a certain place, thousands of young Americans answered their country's call and gave their lives. It will make us remember that war—any war, any time, any place, however necessary and for whatever moral purpose—is about sacrifice and sorrow, not about glory and reward.

The names on the polished black granite wall of the Vietnam Veterans Memorial, seemingly endless as they move away line after line from the center, are a metaphor for the dead of all American wars. I was in the Second World War. Two of my best friends, my boyhood buddies, died in that war.

The first time I saw the Vietnam Veterans Memorial, I was overwhelmed by an impulse to look for their names on the wall: Tom Bulwer and Ralph Corey. Why shouldn't their names be there? In my heart they were there.

◆ Jan Scruggs and Maya Lin Today

J AN SCRUGGS was twenty-nine years old when he began seriously to pursue the idea of a national Vietnam Veterans Memorial, thirty-two when the memorial was built and dedicated. Maya Lin was twenty-one, still a student at Yale, when she conceived the design for the memorial Scruggs's work made possible. She was twenty-two when the memorial was dedicated. As I gathered the material for this book, I found myself wondering what a person does after he or she has accomplished something so awesome at such an early age. The Vietnam Veterans Memorial might have been a fitting capstone to a career for either Jan Scruggs or Maya Lin. What next?

The first time I talked to Jan Scruggs, I saw that the question of the future was very much on his mind. He was still president of the Vietnam Veterans Memorial Fund, but that is a volunteer, unpaid position. The purpose of the Fund now is to add names to the memorial if new deaths are confirmed, to take care of repairs, and to conduct ceremonies at the memorial. For his full time work Scruggs was now executive director of the National Law Enforcement Officers' Memorial Fund, an organization to plan and collect funds for a memorial honoring officers of the law. James J. Kilpatrick wrote in one of his syndicated newspaper columns that law officers were fortunate to have Scruggs directing their memorial organization.

But Scruggs was already planning ahead. "You can't spend your life building memorials," he said.

He told me that he would soon enter the University of Maryland as a law student. I calculated that Scruggs would be something over forty years old when he got his law degree.

"It's a long haul," I said.

Scruggs smiled. "It's something I've decided I want to do," he said. "If I've learned anything, it's that having an idea is only a start. Carrying it out is what counts. I've learned how to carry out an idea."

No one who knows the story of the Vietnam Veterans Memorial would argue with that.

MAYA LIN graduated from Yale with her degree in architecture in 1986. When I talked to her a year after graduation, she was working for an architectural firm in New York, putting in her time as an apprentice so that she could receive her architect's license. She was working on some new concepts in small residential housing. She lives in a loft on the lower East Side—the only place in New York she could afford a loft, she said—where she has room to spread out her art designs.

"My interest in art is still strong," she said. "I have a commission for an art work in Cincinnati that I will start soon."

She told me that she had also designed some theatrical sets and had written an article for *The New Republic*. "I want to write more," she said, "but there is so much to do."

I had the clear impression of someone bursting with ideas and energy, a young professional who didn't for a minute think that her great work was already behind her.

"Some of my colleagues question my commitment to architecture," she said, "because of my interest in art. But I do want to be an architect. Architecture is a very male-dominated profession, but I intend to succeed in it."

Architecture, I thought, make way for one very talented young woman.

◆ Facts About the Vietnam Veterans Memorial

Location: Constitution Gardens on the Mall, Washington, D.C.

Dedication: November 13, 1982

Designer: Maya Ying Lin

Wall: Each half of the wall is 246.75 feet long, combined length of 493.50 feet. Each segment is made of 70 panels. At their intersection, the highest point, they are 10.1 feet high; they taper to a width of 8 inches at their extremities. Granite for the wall came from southern India.

Names: The wall contains 58,175 names (as of October, 1990). The largest panels have 137 lines of names; the smallest panels have but one line. There are five names on each line. The names (and other words) on the wall are 0.53 inches high and 0.015 inches deep.

In addition to the names of the men and women killed or missing in the Vietnam War, the following words are inscribed on the memorial:

IN HONOR OF THE MEN AND WOMEN OF
THE ARMED FORCES OF THE UNITED
STATES WHO SERVED IN THE VIETNAM
WAR. THE NAMES OF THOSE WHO GAVE
THEIR LIVES AND OF THOSE WHO REMAIN
MISSING ARE INSCRIBED IN THE ORDER
THEY WERE TAKEN FROM US.

OUR NATION HONORS THE COURAGE,
SACRIFICE AND DEVOTION TO DUTY AND
COUNTRY OF ITS VIETNAM VETERANS.
THIS MEMORIAL WAS BUILT WITH
PRIVATE CONTRIBUTIONS FROM
THE AMERICAN PEOPLE.
NOVEMBER 11, 1982.

Statue: The statue of the servicemen was sculpted by Frederick Hart. It is cast in bronze and is 7 feet in height. The statue was dedicated on November 11, 1984.

Stamp: On November 10, 1984, the U.S. Postal Service issued a 20¢ stamp commemorating the Vietnam Veterans Memorial.

◆ Bibliography

Brende, Joel Osler and Erwin Randolph Parson. *Vietnam Veterans: the Road to Recovery.* New York: Plenum Press, 1985.

Ezell, Edward Clinton (Introduction and narration). *Reflections on the Wall: The Vietnam Veterans Memorial.* Harrisburg, Penna.: Stackpole Books, 1987.

Lawson, Don. *The United States in the Vietnam War.* New York: Thomas Y. Crowell, 1981.

Mabie, Margot C.J. *Vietnam There and Here.* New York: Holt, Rinehart, and Winston, 1985.

Scruggs, Jan C. and Joel L. Swerdlow. *To Heal a Nation: The Vietnam Veterans Memorial.* New York: Harper and Row, 1985.

"Maya Lin and the Great Call of China," by Phil McCombs, *The Washington Post,* January 3, 1982.

"Vietnam Memorial: America Remembers," *National Geographic,* May, 1985.

"The Wall," by Christopher Buckley, *Esquire,* September, 1985.

◆ Index

The Author

Brent Ashabranner has written widely on American social history and complex social issues for young readers. Among his award-winning books are *The New Americans: Changing Patterns in U.S. Immigration, To Live in Two Worlds: American Indian Youth Today,* and *Dark Harvest: Migrant Farmworkers in America.*

Mr. Ashabranner spent a number of years working as an education advisor in developing countries for the Agency for International Development (AID). He was director of Peace Corps programs in Nigeria and India and later was deputy director of the Peace Corps in Washington, D.C. He has also lived in the Philippines and Indonesia while working for The Ford Foundation.

Mr. Ashabranner now lives in Williamsburg, Virginia, where he devotes all of his time to writing.

The Photographer

Jennifer Ashabranner is the daughter of Brent Ashabranner. A freelance photographer, she also supervises a photographic laboratory in the Fairfax County, Virginia, recreation program. During the late 1950s and early 1960s, Ms. Ashabranner lived with her parents in Ethiopia, Libya, Nigeria, and India and attended school in those countries. Capturing photographic impressions of Africa and Asia stimulated her interest in photography.

101